Finders, Keepers

Written by Lynette Evans
Illustrated by Daniel Rudnicki

My name is Jonah. I live on the Caribbean island of Cuba. Hurricanes that form over the warm waters of the Caribbean Sea have always been dangerous for ships traveling near the jagged coral reefs in this region. In my country, there are many colorful tales about shipwrecks, pirates, and sunken treasure.

Contents

Look for the **Thinking Cap**.
When you see this picture, you will find
a problem to think about and write about.

Sunken Treasure

Galleons of Gold

Havana, Cuba: September 4, 1622

There was great excitement among the soldiers, officers, sailors, and passengers of the Spanish fleet. We were at last setting sail for Spain. The 28 mighty galleons were packed with treasures from the New World. The holds were heavy with gold and emeralds from Columbia, pearls from Venezuela, and silver from Peru and Mexico.

No ship was more heavily loaded than the *Nuestra Señora de Atocha*. The magnificent warship looked like a floating castle as it brought up the rear of the fleet. It was perfect weather, and the *Atocha*'s square sails were billowing in the wind.

Although we were setting sail later than planned, we knew that the King of Spain would be well pleased with our cargo of riches. We had so much treasure aboard that it took nearly two months to load the holds before departure.

galleon a large sailing ship with three or more masts used from the 1400s to the 1700s

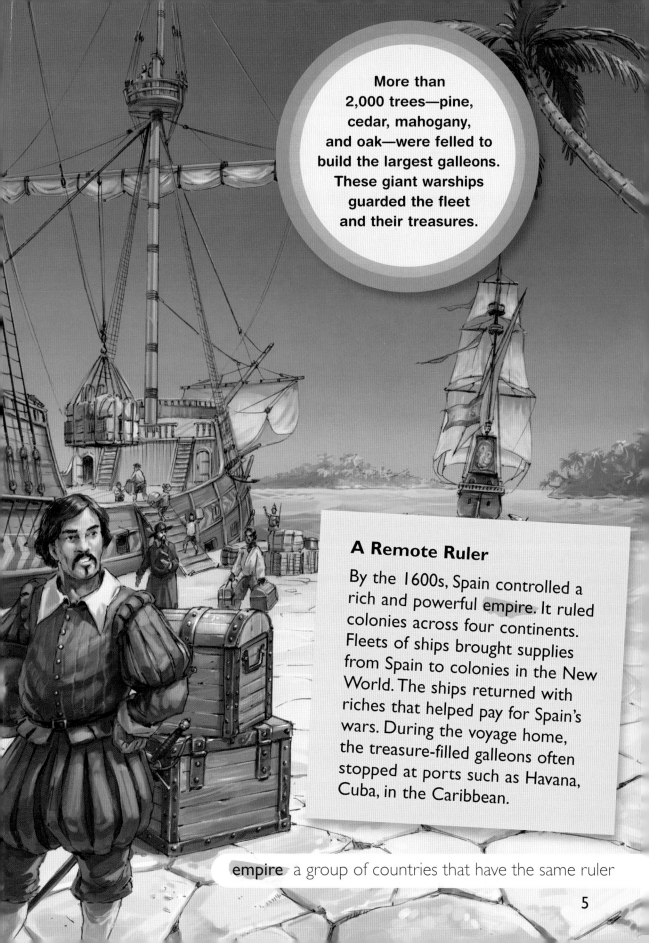

More than 2,000 trees—pine, cedar, mahogany, and oak—were felled to build the largest galleons. These giant warships guarded the fleet and their treasures.

A Remote Ruler

By the 1600s, Spain controlled a rich and powerful empire. It ruled colonies across four continents. Fleets of ships brought supplies from Spain to colonies in the New World. The ships returned with riches that helped pay for Spain's wars. During the voyage home, the treasure-filled galleons often stopped at ports such as Havana, Cuba, in the Caribbean.

empire a group of countries that have the same ruler

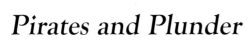

Pirates and Plunder

Many wealthy passengers strolled above decks. A total of 265 people were aboard the *Atocha* for the voyage home to Spain. Each of us knew that the route through the Caribbean was full of danger. Pirate ships lurked in hidden bays, and pirates had **plundered** many a galleon along the way.

There was little doubt that we were safe aboard the *Atocha*, however. She was the pride of the Spanish military. The mighty warship had been built to guard the wealth of the empire and to defend the fleet from enemy attack.

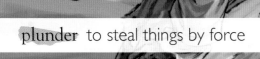

plunder to steal things by force

Shiver Me Timbers!

Pirates have been around for as long as ships have been sailing the seas. During the 1500s and 1600s, Spanish treasure ships were prime targets. The waters and islands of the Caribbean became a popular hangout for pirates. Some were so successful that they became legends. Two fierce pirates of the Caribbean were women. Anne Bonny and Mary Read disguised themselves as men. They were members of the crew of a famous pirate named Calico Jack.

legend a real person about whom larger-than-life stories are told

Wild Wind and Waves

Florida Straits: September 5, 1622

Sometimes danger comes out of the blue. It turns out that we did not need to fear the attacks of pirates, but instead the terrible forces of nature. After only two days at sea, our hopes of a fair-weather voyage were dashed. The galleons began to roll violently on wind-whipped seas. Clouds and heavy rain blackened the sky. Before long, we found ourselves in the fury of a fast-moving hurricane. The fleet was scattered in all directions. Wild winds pushed the *Atocha* and three other galleons toward the Florida Keys and dangerous coral reefs. People hurried to shelter below deck, and many fell to their knees in prayer.

Did You Know?

Hurricane is a Caribbean word for "big wind." Hurricanes get their energy from warm, tropical waters. They commonly form over the Caribbean Sea and the Gulf of Mexico.

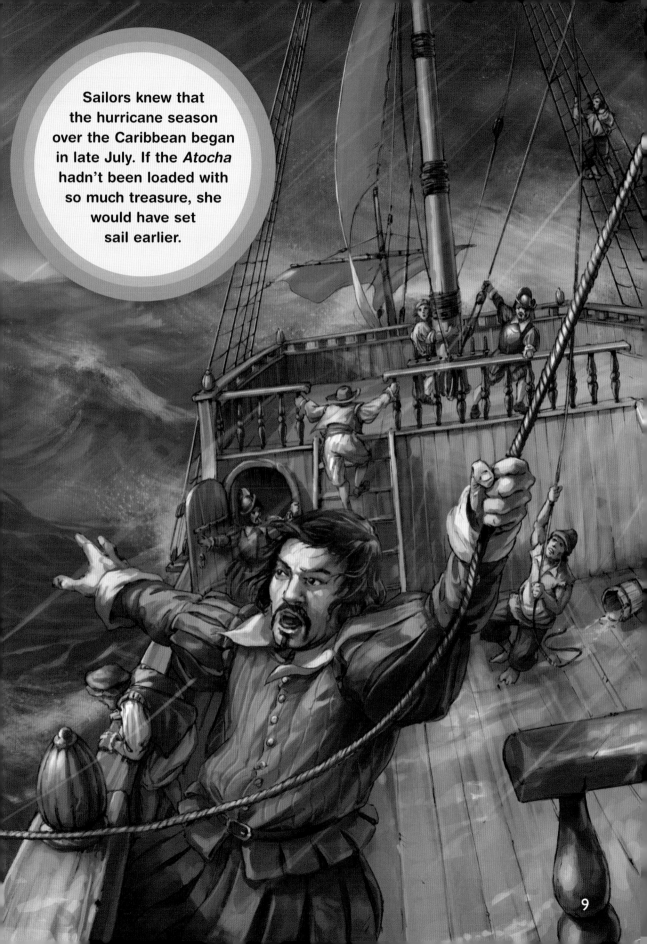

Sailors knew that the hurricane season over the Caribbean began in late July. If the *Atocha* hadn't been loaded with so much treasure, she would have set sail earlier.

Shipwrecked!

Key West, Florida: September 6, 1622

The waves rose like mountains before us,
and the ships plunged and lurched in the sea,
tossed about like the mere toys of children.
We watched in horror as the galleon *Santa
Margarita* was hurled across a low-lying atoll.
The ship broke apart, and its pieces were
cruelly thrown into the shallows beyond.

Then it was our turn. The *Atocha*'s once
lofty sails had been ripped to shreds in
the fierce winds. Her wooden masts and
crossbeams were smashed in the storm's
fury, until only splintered stumps remained.
Now the *Atocha* drifted helplessly toward the
jagged reefs. Then she rose high on a wave
and was hurled violently onto the sharp coral.

With a gaping hole in her bow, there was
no doubt that the great galleon was going
down. Through the noise and darkness
of the storm, I held onto the stump of
a mast with all the strength I had left.
I thought I would surely not live
to see another day.

atoll a chain of small coral islands
        that circles a lagoon

U.S.A.

ATLANTIC OCEAN

Florida

Gulf of Mexico

Atocha wreck site

CUBA

Caribbean Sea

Only three sailors and two slaves survived to tell the tale of the *Atocha*. The mizzenmast was the only part of the wreck that stayed briefly above water.

mizzenmast a mast near the mainmast in a ship

Lost, but Not Forgotten

With the sinking of the Spanish fleet and the heavily-laden galleon the *Atocha* during a fierce hurricane over the Caribbean in 1622, the war plans of a faraway nation were wrecked. The fortune of the fleet was scattered far and wide, across 50 miles of ocean floor.

For 60 years after the disaster, Spain sent divers to recover the lost treasure. However, without breathing equipment, the search time beneath the ocean waves was limited by how long the divers could hold their breath.

However, now with the invention of scuba diving equipment, divers can at last explore shipwrecks lying in deep water. The treasure of the *Atocha* has lain hidden and undisturbed for more than 350 years. But it has not been forgotten. Will a new generation of treasure seekers succeed in putting science and technology together so they can strike gold?

The ocean floor in and around the Caribbean is littered with wrecks, riches, and artifacts from the past. Time and technology have turned dreams of finding these treasures into reality. But who has the right to search for treasures in the sea, and should people be allowed to keep what they find?

Put On Your Thinking Cap

Write down your thoughts so that you can discuss these questions with a classmate.

1. What challenges might be involved in recovering a shipwreck?

2. What value, besides financial, do artifacts from shipwrecks have?

3. Should important objects found in the sea belong to those who find them, to the country nearest to where they are found, or to the country from which they originally came?

Scuba stands for *self-contained underwater breathing apparatus*. When Jacques Cousteau (right) and Emile Gagnan invented this technology in 1943, it enabled divers to breathe underwater for up to an hour. At last, people could explore wrecks that were previously out of reach.

artifact an object made by people long ago

What's the Problem?

The world is rich with treasures from history. People have found valuable artifacts from ancient cities hidden beneath the ground. They have found treasures buried deep within pyramids, plunder stashed away in caves, and priceless pieces of the past concealed in the clutter of dusty attics and sheds. Hundreds of years ago, when people found treasure, they often took pieces for themselves and carelessly destroyed other valuable items.

The oldest shipwrecks can be found in the Mediterranean Sea. However, there are shipwrecks in all the oceans of the world. The Caribbean is especially rich in wrecks and artifacts because of the overloaded, leaky treasure ships that passed through the region long ago.

At first, divers could search only in shallow waters by holding their breath. When diving suits were invented in the 1800s, people began to dive in deeper water. They rummaged through wreck sites and took what they wanted to sell. Over the years, many valuable shipwrecks were looted.

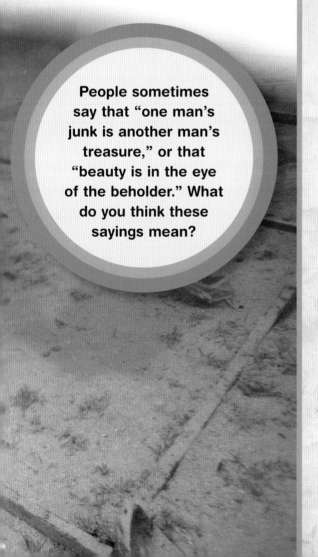

People sometimes say that "one man's junk is another man's treasure," or that "beauty is in the eye of the beholder." What do you think these sayings mean?

Marine Archaeology

Archaeologists are scientists who study cultures of the past by finding and examining ancient objects. During the 1960s, people began to realize the importance of exploring underwater sites slowly and carefully. Laws were created, and the science of marine archaeology was born.

Marine archaeologists study shipwrecks because they are like time capsules of information about people and cultures of the past. Marine archaeologists are interested in far more than treasure. They study and document every object they find at a wreck site.

A Treasure Hunt

"Once you have seen the ocean bottom paved with gold coins, you'll never forget it!"—Mel Fisher, 1922–1998

Mel Fisher said that he caught the treasure bug as a boy when he read Robert Louis Stevenson's famous adventure story, *Treasure Island*. He remembered making his first diving helmet out of a bucket, a length of hose, and a bicycle pump. As an adult, he formed a diving company called Treasure Salvors.

In 1969, after many spectacular discoveries of wrecked Spanish galleons in and around the Caribbean, Fisher decided to search for the lost treasure of the *Atocha*. His quest took him and his team of divers, geographers, and historians 16 years. In 1985, their hard work and persistence paid off. The divers discovered treasure and valuable artifacts that helped historians create a picture of the past.

Mel and Deo Fisher display some of the gold they found while excavating a wreck site in the Marquesas Keys, off the Florida coast.

There was hot debate over Mel Fisher's discovery and salvage of the *Atocha*. Some people thought that the team cared only about the riches they would gain from the wreck. They believed that important objects from the past, such as pottery, were carelessly buried during the salvage operation. However, Mel Fisher's team say that they valued everything from the wreck and excavated the site using careful, scientific methods.

Do you think that pottery, statues, and other objects from long ago should be valued as much as gold and silver? Why or why not?

Several bronze cannons were excavated from the *Atocha*. They carry the royal crest of Philip III of Spain. The cannons are now on display at the Mel Fisher Maritime Museum. The *Atocha* may have carried about 40 tons of gold and silver. Today, it would be worth more than $100 million.

Finding treasure underwater is not just a matter of "finders keepers." Many countries lay claim to treasure found in their territorial waters, which is usually the area within about 12 miles of the coast.

excavate to search for objects from the past by removing sand or earth

Scientists Strike Gold!

Persistence paid off well for a team of archaeologists and other scientists aboard the research ship *Odyssey Explorer*. After more than a decade of searching, the Odyssey team found the wreck of a Civil War era steamship, the *S.S. Republic*. She lies upright, nearly 1,700 feet beneath the waves. The site is about 100 miles off the coast of Georgia, where the ship sank in a powerful hurricane more than 140 years ago.

The team used a remotely operated vehicle, or ROV, to excavate the wreck. The ROV has a video camera and special claws to retrieve objects. Dishes, bottles, and other artifacts from the Civil War era have been retrieved from the ocean floor. One day, however, the Odyssey crew struck gold! They found a treasure trove of coins spilling from the rim of a buried barrel. These special coins are thought to be worth millions of dollars.

People are still searching for shipwrecks and discovering riches and relics from the past. Advances in technology continue to allow more wrecks to be found and explored.

Underwater Exploration

Today, sonar devices, cameras, and computers allow archaeologists and treasure seekers to search the ocean depths without even getting their feet wet! Salvage teams can operate from the comfort of sophisticated research ships. High-tech submersibles and ROVs can reach parts of the ocean that were once inaccessible.

Scientists from around the world explore marine life at the Perry Institute for Marine Science in the Caribbean. Former marine researcher John H. Perry Jr. is shown here in his underwater research habitat, which he reached with his personal submarine.

submersible a small underwater craft used for deep-sea research

19

Wrecks Around the World

Treasure Found

AMOY, CHINA – The *Tek Sing*, a huge Chinese trading ship, set sail from China in 1822. Her cargo consisted of more than 350,000 pieces of fine china. The ship struck a reef near Indonesia and sank. Of the 1,800 people on board, only about 200 survived. The wreck remained lost for more than 170 years.

Lost Gold

NEW JERSEY, UNITED STATES – In 1698, pirates captured a Moorish merchant ship. A plaque from the ship was found off the coast of New Jersey, but the loot has never been found.

No Ship, No Pay

TSUSHIMA STRAIT, JAPAN – Russian cruiser *Admiral Nakhimov* was sunk by a Japanese torpedo in 1905, during the Russo-Japanese War. The ship's cargo of gold coins, gold ingots, and platinum ingots was meant as payroll for crew members of the Russian fleet.

A Famous Wreck

NEWFOUNDLAND, CANADA – The *Titanic* is perhaps the most famous shipwreck in the world. In 1912, the luxury liner struck an iceberg on its first voyage. It was traveling from England to America. The *Titanic* sank two-and-a-half miles beneath the North Atlantic Ocean. More than 1,500 people lost their lives. Many years later, Dr. Robert Ballard and Jean-Louis Michel discovered the wreck on the ocean floor. After much debate, the *Titanic* was declared a memorial to the people who lost their lives on that cold, dark night almost a century ago. The wreck will no longer be disturbed.

Gold Cape

SOUTH AFRICA – In 1782, the British ship *Grosvenor* struck a reef about 700 miles northeast of Cape Town, South Africa, on its way from Sri Lanka to Britain. It sank with a cargo of gold, silver, and jewels said to be worth millions. The treasure has not yet been located.

What's Your Opinion?

Marine archaeologists and treasure seekers need to consider all the issues involved in recovering shipwrecks before they start searching. It is important that other people think about the issues, too.

- Who should own the finds? Why?

- What is more important: becoming rich or carefully and slowly uncovering information about the past? Explain your opinion.

- Should the finds be sold to private collectors or given to museums? Why?

- If the finders are not allowed to be keepers, will anyone search for the remaining wrecks, or will they be lost forever? Explain your opinion.

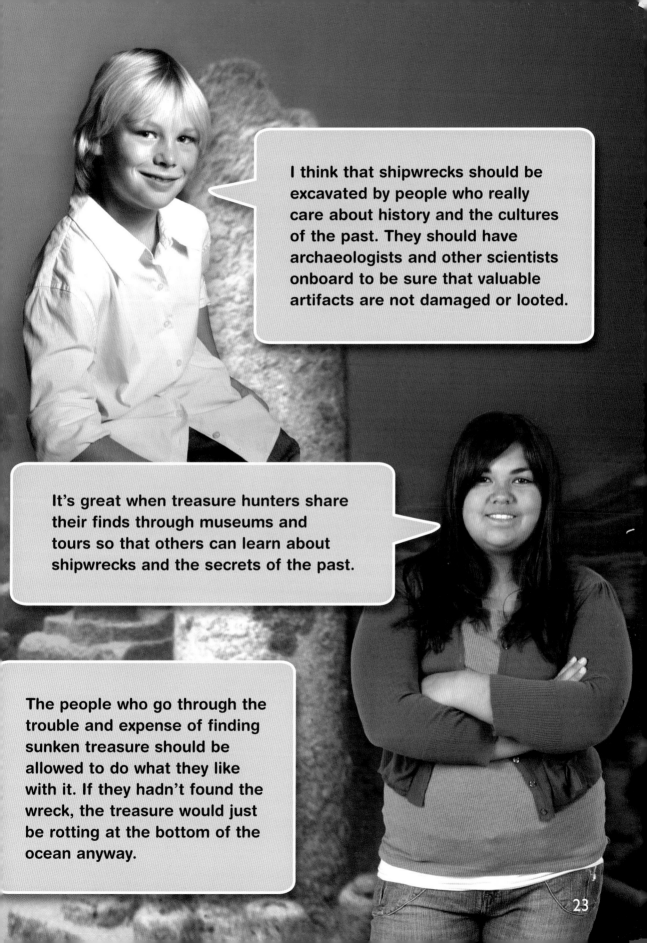

I think that shipwrecks should be excavated by people who really care about history and the cultures of the past. They should have archaeologists and other scientists onboard to be sure that valuable artifacts are not damaged or looted.

It's great when treasure hunters share their finds through museums and tours so that others can learn about shipwrecks and the secrets of the past.

The people who go through the trouble and expense of finding sunken treasure should be allowed to do what they like with it. If they hadn't found the wreck, the treasure would just be rotting at the bottom of the ocean anyway.

Think Tank

1 Imagine that you were a member of a team of archaeologists on a shipwreck excavation. What would you do with the artifacts you found? Why?

2 People sometimes say, "It takes money to make money." How do you think this saying might apply to the recovery of shipwrecks?

3 People are not allowed to dig up Egyptian tombs and sell the jewelry. Should people be allowed to sell artifacts from ancient shipwrecks?

Find out more about treasures of the past and the work marine archaeologists do all over the world. Visit **www.researchit.org** on the Web.

Index